Etosha National Park

Blue wildebeest

© in photographs: Uwe Jäschke, Monica Spall, Bryony van der Merwe, Tatum van der Merwe, fotolio.com, Adobe Stock (Sam D'Cruz, Ward)
© Map: Prof. Dr. U. Jäschke, University of Applied Science, Dresden, Germany
© Front cover photograph: ondrejprosicky/Adobe Stock
© Back cover JohanSwanepoel/Adobe Stock

All rights reserved. No part of this publication may be reproduced, or transmitted in any form or by any means electronic, mechanical, photocopying, recording or otherwise, without the prior written permission from the publishers. Whilst every effort has been made to ensure that the information in this publication is correct, the publishers are not liable for any incorrect information.

Published in 2020

ISBN 9798606003129

Published by:

Heartstone Publishing
S10 3ET, Sheffield, UK
www.heart-stone-house.com
admin@heart-stone-house.com

Projects & Promotions
P.O. Box 152, Swakopmund, Namibia
Tel: +264-81-4016888
proprom.monica@gmail.com

Black-faced impala

Yellow mongoose

Welcome to Etosha

Welcome to our favourite place in Namibia! Despite the arid and unforgiving environment, there is a huge variety of wildlife roaming Etosha National Park. Each season brings its own unique changes in viewing possibilities.

We hope that the information and advice in this guide will help you make the most of your journey through this park and increase your opportunities of spectacular and memorable sightings.

Etosha should not be rushed. Take your time, the park is so vast and there is much to discover. You will see more, and enjoy your experience more, if you plan your routes and allow the time to enjoy each sighting and landscape along the way.

This guide has been compiled by Namibians who visit Etosha on a regular basis. Our maps are continuously updated by our team of cartographers.

Burchell's zebra

African elephant

Lion

Cape hare

Giraffe

Common ostrich, female right, male left

Contents

Reasons to visit Etosha 4
History of Etosha 6
  The Etosha Pan 6
Different ways to experience Etosha............................7
  Self-drive 7
  Self-drive/guided tour mix 7
  Organised tour... 7
Planning your self-drive holiday 8
  Best time to visit 8
  Length of stay... 8
  Some packing suggestions 9
Getting to Etosha 10
Park rules.. 11
Accommodation options 12
  Benefits of staying inside/outside the park 12
  Resorts and facilities 13
Planning your game drive 14
  Game viewing tips..15
  Waterhole watching 16
  Night viewing 16
  Popular waterholes 17
  Best viewing times 18
  Suggested routes 19
Birding in Etosha..22
Animal adaptations 24
Spotting the difference 26
Animal identification 29
  Mammals 29
  Birds..33
  Reptiles...41
Map of Etosha 42
Index 45

Blue wildebeest

Reasons to visit Etosha

There is nowhere quite like Etosha. A vast game park offering an amazing variety of animals despite the arid environment. Ironically, the fact that there are no rivers in the park actually improves game sighting opportunities as animals are forced to gather at the waterholes.

Abundance of game

Etosha is home to 4 of the Big 5 (elephant, lion, leopard and two species of rhino). Other mammal species include giraffe, a variety of antelope, the endangered black-faced impala and cheetah, bat-eared and Cape foxes, and two species of hyaena and zebra. Etosha is home to 113 mammal species, including the largest population of black rhino in the world.

Cheetah

Spectacular landscapes

There are many diverse landscapes in the park. Sunsets are awe-inspiring and the night sky is filled with stars. The Etosha pan makes for dramatic views, both in winter (when it's a striking dry white landscape) and in summer (when after heavy rains it fills with water and attracts many bird species).

Common warthog

Birding

Etosha is a bird-lovers' paradise, with over 340 recorded species.

Epic game drives

Visitors rarely leave Etosha disappointed. Follow our tips in this book to help you experience spectacular sightings on your game drive.

Africa for beginners

Namibia is known as 'Africa for beginners' because it has good infrastructure, is easy to navigate and is considered a lot safer than its neighbouring countries. However, take precautions against petty crime.

Accommodation variety

From upmarket lodges to inexpensive campsites, both inside and outside the park, Etosha has something to suit your style and budget (see pages 12-13).

Affordability

Etosha is considered to be one of the most affordable game park options in Africa.

Easy to get to

Etosha is an easy drive from either Windhoek or Swakopmund. The main roads to Etosha are tarred and well-maintained. There are also light aircraft options, allowing you to fly directly to the park.

Malaria free

Etosha is malaria free during the winter months. During the rainy season, when there are plenty of mosquitoes, most international health organisations advise taking precautions such as prophylaxis.

Bronze-winged courser

Southern yellow-billed hornbill

Burchell's zebra

African elephant

History of Etosha

Etosha National Park is located in north-western Namibia. It was proclaimed a game reserve on 22 March 1907 and covers an area of 22,270km².

Etosha National Park was named after the Etosha Pan, which is located within the park. In Oshivambo, the word 'Etosha' means 'Great White Place'.

This national park is considered to be one of the best game viewing locations in the world, attracting visitors from all over the world.

Due to the arid environment, wildlife rely on the waterholes scattered throughout the park, which gives incredible game viewing opportunities.

The Etosha Pan

The Etosha Pan is a vast open expanse of 130km long and up to 50km wide. It is the largest salt pan in Africa and can be seen from space. The pan was originally a lake but changes in the earth's climate altered the course of the rivers that once fed it. During a good rainy season, the pan becomes a shallow lake, attracting a wide variety of wetland birds. There is very little vegetation growing in the pan, except for some grass species.

Different ways to experience Etosha

There are a variety of options when it comes to exploring Etosha. Self-driving is popular as the park is well sign-posted and easy to navigate. Depending on your budget and preferences, you might prefer to travel with your own personal travel guide.

Self-drive

Etosha is a relatively easy drive from Windhoek or Swakopmund (see page 10). Once in the park, the area is mostly flat and the gravel roads usually in fairly good condition (except during the rainy season).

Pros
- You can stay at a sighting for as long as you want to.
- You have the freedom of deciding when and where to drive.
- You are in charge of your own itinerary.
- It is a cheaper option.

Cons
- You might miss some spectacular sightings due to inexperience.
- Driving around the park can be exhausting.
- You are responsible for everything.

Organised tour

Etosha safari tour options include joining a tour group or booking your own personal travel guide. There are many variables to choose from depending on your needs, time constraints, preferences and budget.

Pros
- Limited stress, as someone else takes care of everything.
- The knowledge and experience of the tour guide can expand your insights and sighting opportunities.

Cons
- You are locked into a pre-existing time-frame.
- You might find the constant companionship invasive.
- You can't be spontaneous.
- Your accommodation options are more limited.

Self-drive plus guided game drives

This option involves driving to Etosha on your own, staying where you choose, and signing up for a few guided game drives.

Guided game drives are available at most camps inside the park (and is the only way to experience a night game drive). On the downside, tours are often fully booked in season and can be expensive.

Planning your self-drive holiday

Planning your safari can seem like a daunting prospect, especially if you haven't been to Namibia before. Hopefully the following steps will help ease your stress.

Best time to visit

Etosha essentially has two seasons: the dry season (June – October) and the rainy season (November – May).

The dry season is by far the best time for viewing animals as the park is very dry and animals are forced to drink from waterholes. This makes their behaviour fairly predictable and you can get incredible sightings by waiting at waterholes. The sparse vegetation also makes animals easier to spot. However, accommodation is more expensive during the dry season and needs to be booked further in advance. This is also the main holiday season for Europeans, and therefore park is full of visitors which can detract from the peace and tranquillity usually experienced when spending time in Etosha.

The rainy season also offers its own delights. The park is transformed into a green wilderness and after good rains the pan forms a lake which attracts wetland birds such as flamingos. Accommodation is much cheaper, the park is much quieter, but certain roads become flooded and impassable.

The dry season

The rainy season

Length of stay

Don't rush Etosha. It is best to spend at least three nights here in order to appreciate all Etosha has to offer.

When to book

You need to book your holiday to Etosha many months in advance, especially is you plan to visit during the dry season, as accommodation is often fully booked closer to the time.

Some packing suggestions

- Thin, light clothing and sun hat
- Sunglasses – the reflection of the sun on the white sand of Etosha can be almost blinding
- Anti-malarials
- Headlamp/torch for getting around the camp at night
- Binoculars
- Comfortable walking shoes
- Closed shoes – especially for walking around the camp at night, to protect your feet from scorpion stings and mosquito bites
- Mobile phone charger and adaptor
- Water and snacks
- Power adaptors – You might need to bring an adapter with. It is best to check this out before travelling.
- Sunblock and after-sun lotion
- Toilet paper
- Wet wipes
- Insect repellent
- Map and guidebooks
- Small first aid kit which should include some basic supplies such as painkillers, aspirin, plasters, bandages, antihistamine or hydrocortisone cream, antiseptic, rehydration sachets, car sickness and diarrhoea tablets
- Moisturising lotion and lip salve
- Great music to listen

Camera

Take a decent camera with and at least two lenses. A tripod is recommended for night photography at the resort waterholes. A lens cleaning kit is also recommended as Etosha can be very dusty. Take plenty of memory cards as well as your camera battery charger (make sure you have the right adapter). If you are using a telephoto or zoom lens, bring something soft to rest the lens on when taking photographs out of the window.

Food and drink in Etosha

The three main camps (Okaukuejo, Halali and Namutoni) serve buffet meals. The shops sell crisps, ice cream, soft drinks and other basic supplies. Campers can stock up on meat, wood for the fire and some basic vegetables and fruit. The variety isn't large, so if you aren't planning on eating all your meals in the restaurants, it is advisable to shop at a grocery store before entering Etosha. Okaukuejo has a kiosk which sells toasted sandwiches and the like.

Wi-Fi

Wi-Fi is available at all the resorts inside Etosha as well as accommodation establishments outside the park.

Car accessories

Make sure you have a spare tyre and jack, and that you know how to change a tyre.

Getting to Etosha

If you are driving to Etosha, you'll find the main tar roads are well-maintained.

There are four gates by which to enter the park:

- Andersson Gate (via C38 in the south),
- Von Lindequist Gate (via B1 in the east),
- King Nehale gate (via B1 in the north) and
- Galton Gate (via C35 in the west).

Choose the best gate by which to enter by taking into account where you are driving from, and where you will be staying. There are several accommodation options both inside and outside the park (see pages 12-13).

Please note that all gates into Etosha are closed between sunset and sunrise. Visitors are charged an entrance fee.

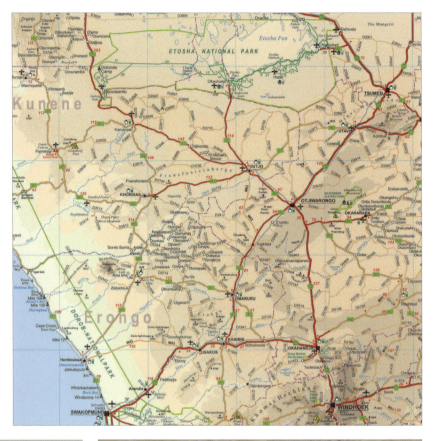

Distance table

Dolomite								
229	Halali							
288	75	Namutoni						
173	56	115	Okaukuejo					
49	196	260	127	Olifantsrus				
352	139	64	179	306	Onkoshi			
336	256	288	190	319	352	Otjiwarongo		
520	578	659	561	503	723	371	Swakopmund	
518	182	107	345	500	171	181	522	Tsumeb
626	501	533	435	568	597	245	356	426	Windhoek

Black-backed jackal

Park rules

- Park hours: sunrise to sunset.
- Report to reception on arrival.
- Permits can be bought at the Ministry of Environment and Tourism counter.
- Accommodation check-in 12h00, check-out 10h00.
- Speed limit: 60 km/h in the park and 20 km/h in the resorts.
- No off-road driving is permitted.
- Excessive noise is not allowed.
- When on a game drive, remain in the vehicle at all times, except in demarcated areas.
- Do not open the vehicle doors, lean out of the windows or sunroofs or climb on top of your vehicle when inside the park.
- Wildlife always have right of way. Keep a good distance from animals. Do not threaten them, harass them or interact with them in any way.
- In order to drive in the park, you must have a valid drivers' license and have it with you when driving.
- Obey all signs in the park.
- Be courteous to other drivers and visitors.
- Be quiet at waterholes.
- Night driving is prohibited. You need to leave the park, or return to your resort, before the gates close. There are severe penalties if you are caught driving inside the park after the gates have closed.

Animals always have right of way.

Road surface

Most of the roads in Etosha are gravel. It is possible to transverse Etosha with a normal sedan car. Most road surfaces are fairly straightforward to drive on. However, the road surface can sometimes be corrugated or damaged. During heavy rains some roads become flooded. Many recommend a 4x4 vehicle which has a higher ground clearance and manages tricky driving conditions better.

Accommodation options

There are accommodation options available both inside and outside Etosha National Park. The camps inside the park are all run by Namibia Wildlife Resorts.

Benefits of staying in the park

Floodlit waterholes
Many animals frequent the floodlit waterholes at the resorts. This makes for very interesting night viewing opportunities. Black rhino and elephant often drink at Okaukuejo waterhole at night.

Elephant at Okaukuejo floodlit waterhole

Out and about earlier
One of the best times for game-viewing is early morning. The main benefit of staying inside the park is that you can be out on a game drive as soon as the resort gates open. There is often a queue of vehicles lining up to enter the park when the gates open in the morning. Each vehicle needs to fill in paperwork, so the queue often moves slowly and this reduces your early morning game drive opportunities.

Benefits of staying outside the park

Government owned accommodation versus private lodges
Because the resorts in Etosha are all run by a government-owned parastatal, there are certain restrictions, irritations and times when things just don't work properly. The many upmarket lodges in the area will offer you a very different experience, where you'll feel more like a guest and have a bigger and better range of choices.

Amenities inside the park

Day visits can make use of the information centre, toilets, restaurant, shop, kiosk, swimming pool and petrol station available at the resorts. There is a sightings book at reception where visitors report interesting animal sightings, making a note of the date and time. Always check this book when stopping past a resort because it could lead you to an epic sighting. If you've seen something interesting, make your own entry.

Outside of the resorts, the only places you can exit your vehicle inside the park is at the demarcated toilets/picnic sites. These toilets a very basic, and can be quite dirty and smelly. Bring your own toilet paper with.

Resorts and facilities inside the park

Below is an overview of the resorts in Etosha and the facilities they offer. All resorts inside the park are run by Namibia Wildlife Resorts.

Chalets | Camping | Petrol | Restaurant | Kiosk | Swimming pool | Grocery shop | Curio shop | Waterhole | Game drives

Dolomite ☎ 065-685 119
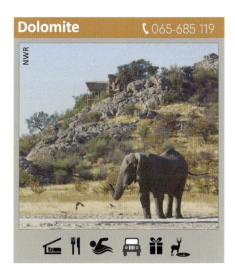

Halali ☎ 067-229 400
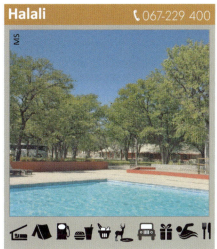

Okaukuejo ☎ 067-229 800

Olifantsrus ☎ 061-285 7200
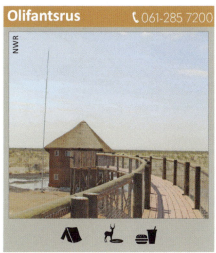

Onkoshi ☎ 085-5502 342
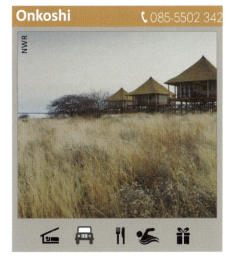

Namutoni ☎ 067-229 300

Planning your game drive

Before setting out on your game drive, it's worthwhile to plan your route. The next few pages give some advice about things to consider.

- When planning your route, bear in mind the condition of the roads and the possibility of spending more time than anticipated at a good sighting. The park is huge, as are the distances between places. It can take 1.5 hours to drive from Okaukuejo to Halali, a distance of only 56km. Keep this in mind when planning how much to do in one day.
- Don't try to cover too much distance at one time. Rather take shorter routes with frequent stops at waterholes.
- Fuel is available at some resorts. See previous page for details.
- Early mornings and evenings are the best viewing and photographic times.
- All resorts have a sighting book at reception. It is advisable to check this book before heading out on your game drive.
- Patience is often rewarded. A waterhole might seem empty when you arrive, but waiting could reveal an elusive animal.
- The slower you drive the more animals you are likely to see.
- Make sure you return to your camp before sunset. As the roads are gravel and driving conditions can be variable, so take this into account when planning your drive.
- If you see other cars stopped on the side of the road, slow down; maybe they have seen something and you can share in their sighting.

Checklist

- ☐ Binoculars
- ☐ Camera equipment
- ☐ Map
- ☐ Bird and wildlife books
- ☐ Insect repellent
- ☐ Sunscreen and hat
- ☐ Cooler box
- ☐ Coffee flask
- ☐ Swimming costume and towel
- ☐ Drinking water and snacks
- ☐ Toilet paper

Game drive tips

Get moving early
Wake up early and be ready to drive at sunrise. Prepare everything you need the night before, so you can be streamlined in the morning and be at the gate when it opens. Many nocturnal animals will be heading home now, after a night of hunting, so keep an eye out for them.

Game sighting book
Each resort has a book where guests may write down which animals they have seen and where. While the location of species changes constantly, these books can be a good indication of what is in the area for the day.

Chat to people
Guides, park and camp staff should be able to give you information about where you might be able to see certain animals. Visitors often share sightings with each other, and listening to what others have seen will give you ideas about which direction to drive next.

Spotting predators
Prey animals can sometimes give away the location of a predator by their actions. For instance, antelope are always alert and are very sensitive to signs of danger. If you see them acting skittish then look at the surrounding area. Giraffe are often the first to spot approaching predators, because of their height.

Take detours
Get off the main road and explore some of the meandering routes.

Keep your gaze moving
Keep a look out under trees and shrubs. Many animals seek shelter from the sun during the heat of the day. Look for shape and movement in the bushes as you drive past.

Circling vultures
Vultures circling in the sky can give away the location of a recent kill.

Lappet-faced vulture

Cheetah

Waterhole watching

During the dry season, animals are forced to drink at waterholes as there is no other water available. This make it easier to predict where and when you'll see certain animals.

Each waterhole has a unique atmosphere and is frequented by different mammals and birds. Most waterholes have areas where you can stop, switch off your engine and wait for game to arrive. Even if the waterhole appears empty when you arrive, waiting quietly can be more rewarding than driving around for hours. Make as little noise as possible while you wait, to respect the other people at the waterhole as well as the animals, which may not venture near if they hear unusual sounds. It is also imperative that you stay inside your vehicle, as tempting as it might be to get out and stretch your legs. If other vehicles are parked at the same waterhole, take a look at where the people are looking. Have they seen something you haven't?

Black-faced impala

Burchell's zebra

Greater kudu

Night viewing

Okaukuejo, Halali and Namutoni each have a floodlit waterhole for night-time viewing.

Okaukuejo's waterhole has the best reputation, with rhino, elephant and lion being frequent visitors. It is not uncommon for visitors to sit watching until the early morning hours.

Black rhino at Okaukuejo waterhole

Popular waterholes

Okaukuejo area

Okondeka: Frequent lion sightings. Herds of antelope and beautiful views over the pan.

Gemsbokvlakte, Olifantsbad, Aus: Herds of antelope. Elephant during dry season. Lion sightings common.

Ombika: 2km from Andersson Gate. Lion, giraffe, elephant and herds of antelope.

Newbrownii: Hyaena in the early morning. Also lion, elephant, rhino and antelope.

Halali area

Moringa (Halali): A good bet for leopard, elephant, rhino and hyaena.

Goas: Leopard and hyaena common in early mornings.

Sueda, Salvadora: Cheetah sightings are often recorded. Very picturesque views over salt pan.

Charitsaub: Frequent cheetah sightings.

Rietfontein: Very scenic. Wide water surface. Variety of animals common, including lion.

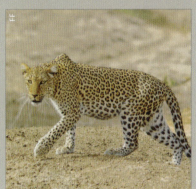

Namutoni area

Klein Namutoni: Giraffe and leopard often seen here.

Chudob: Pretty waterhole. Hyaena often seen swimming in early mornings.

Koinachas: A good spot to see leopard.

Fischer's Pan: A birder's paradise, especially in the rainy season.

Tsumcor: Often giraffe and elephant.

Best viewing times

Early morning
Early morning is the overall best time for game-viewing. Aim to be ready to go as soon as the resort gates open as some nocturnal animals will still be active. Take a flask of coffee with to enjoy at a waterhole.

Midday
Driving in the heat of the day is not always ideal, however, you can get excellent sightings at waterholes. Lunch at one of the resorts, and an afternoon swim, is highly recommended.

Afternoon
Late afternoon is another great time for a game drive. Animals start moving again, after their midday siesta, often heading to waterholes for one last drink. Nocturnal animals are waking up. Always bear in mind how far you are from your resort, so that you can be back before the gates close.

If you are lucky enough to see interesting animals during the heat of the day, chances are that they won't be doing much.

Big cat spotting tips

Lions are widespread in Etosha Look for them near Okondeka, Ombika, Groot Okevi and Rietfontein.

Look for cheetah in the open plains near Charitsaub, Sueda, Salvadora, Leeubron and Twee Palms.

Look for leopard in trees and under bushes near Halali, Goas and Klein Namutoni.

Suggested routes

Here are a few of our favourite routes through Etosha, which often give superb sightings. Each game drive experience is unique and the sightings mentioned below are obviously not guaranteed.

1. Upon entering the park

Ombika, only 2km from Andersson Gate, is a spectacular waterhole at which lion, giraffe, elephant and herds of antelope are often seen.

2. In search of the pride

A trip to **Okondeka** is often rewarded by lion sightings. Many herds of antelope and beautiful views over the pan add to the experience. However, the detour via Adamax, Natco and Leeubron may be disappointing, as these waterholes are often dry, so a u-turn at Okondeka is recommended.

3. Short drive from Okaukuejo

Nebrownii is a great way to start your day. Hyaena are often seen in the early morning. It offers a superb variety of animals, ranging from lion, elephant and rhino, as well as antelope. Check the pipes running beneath the road, as lion cubs and hyaena are often seen there.

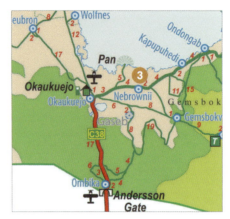

4. Elephant footprints

This drive takes you via **Gemsbokvlakte**, **Olifantsbad** and **Aus** waterholes. Elephant can be seen here during the dry season. This road is often closed during the rainy season.

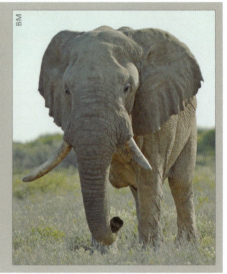

5. The illusive leopard

An early morning drive to **Goas** might reward you with leopard and hyaena sightings. There are two waterholes, so spending some time here offers a variety of different sighting opportunities. If heading to Namutoni, the road via Goas is a nice alternative to the main road.

5. The bird lovers' drive

This drive takes you around **Fischer's Pan**, via the **Twee Palms**, **Aroe**, **Groot Okevi** and **Klein Okevi** waterholes. This is a very scenic route, especially during the rainy season, when pelicans and flamingos can be seen in the water that collects in the pan.

6. Short drives from Namutoni

Klein Namutoni and **Koinachas** are both pretty waterholes with nice character. **Klein Namutoni** is often teaming with wildlife. Leopard are sometimes seen here. **Chudob** is also a stunning waterhole where hyaenas are often seen swimming in the early mornings.

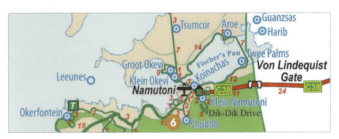

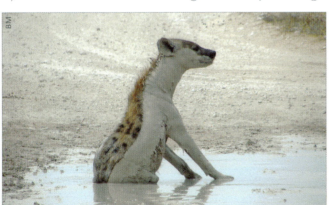

Spotted hyaena

Giraffe

21

Birding in Etosha

Birding in Etosha is a very rewarding experience. Only one third of the 340 species are migratory, so year round there are great sighting opportunities. However, the best time for bird viewing is in the rainy season (November – May), when migrant birds from all over the world come visiting. After good rain, the pan fills with water and creates lakes which attract many wetland bird species.

Flamingos

Flamingos breed in Etosha between December and February. They are possibly the best known migrating species, with almost 30,000 breeding pairs recorded here at a given time. After good rains, they descend upon Fischer's Pan. Both lesser and greater flamingos are found here during breeding season.

A flock of lesser flamingo

Water birds

Waterholes (and lakes in the pan) attract a large number of wetland species as well as waders, cranes, grebes, pelicans, storks and even the African jacana.

Owls

Etosha has eight recorded owl species, from the tiny pearl spotted owlet to the spotted eagle owl. The African and southern white-faced scops-owls are frequently recorded near Halali.

Birds of prey

There are 35 different raptor species including a variety of eagles, vultures and others. From the tiny pygmy falcon to the immense marital eagle.

Pygmy falcon

Kori bustard

Crowned lapwing

Common ostrich

European bee-eater

Spotted eagle owl

Northern black korhaan

Crimson-breasted shrike

Southern pale chanting goshawk

Damara hornbill

African pipit

Red-billed spurfowl

Animal adaptations
African elephant

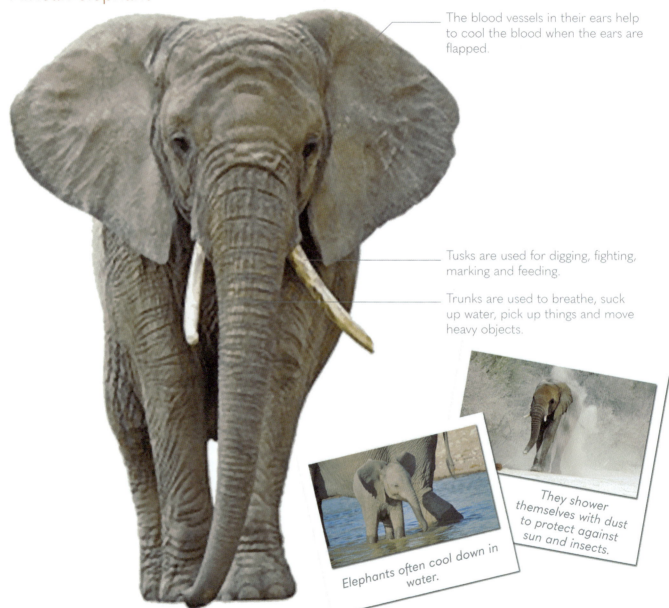

The blood vessels in their ears help to cool the blood when the ears are flapped.

Tusks are used for digging, fighting, marking and feeding.

Trunks are used to breathe, suck up water, pick up things and move heavy objects.

Elephants often cool down in water.

They shower themselves with dust to protect against sun and insects.

Southern oryx

Oryx can raise their body temperature to prevent sweating.

Black and white pattern cools body down.

Powerful horns used for defence.

Capillaries in nose cool down blood.

White belly patch reflects heat from ground to keep the animal cool.

Digs up roots and tubers for water content.

Oryx can survive several months without drinking water.

Bat-eared fox

Large powerful ears used to source prey. Blood vessels in ears help keep fox cool.

Specialised extra teeth for chewing insects. Lower jawbone designed to open and close rapidly.

Claws designed for digging.

These foxes travel up to 12km each night searching for food.

Spotting the difference

Leopard

Leopards are powerful. They hunt by stealth. Their front feet are bigger to carry the weight of heavy carcasses. They have retractable claws which are used when climbing. Often seen in areas with cover.

Large neck and head

Rosette markings

Robust build

Tail is tubular in shape

Cheetah

Cheetah are built for speed. Every part of their anatomy is carefully designed to allow for them to accelerate and reach high speeds quickly. Their back feet are bigger to allow for quick acceleration. They have non-retractable claws for traction when turning at high speed. They hunt in groups, and their speed is therefore essential in chasing and taking down prey. They cannot maintain their speed for long periods of time. Often seen on open plains.

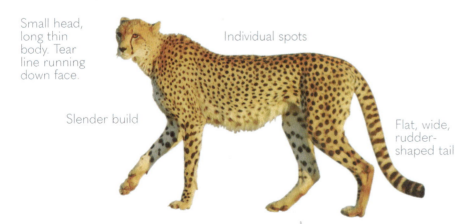

Small head, long thin body. Tear line running down face.

Individual spots

Slender build

Flat, wide, rudder-shaped tail

Steenbok
- Large ears
- White patch
- Preorbital gland
- White patch

Common duiker
- Tuft of dark hair
- Black band
- Preorbital gland

Damara dik-dik
- Tuft of orange-brown hair
- Bulbous nose
- Small nostrils

Spotting the difference

Black rhinoceros

Smaller in size, shorter and more compact. Back has deep arch.

The black rhino is a browser. Mouth designed for feeding on leaves, using pointed lip to hold thorny trees. Head mostly held high.

Ears rounded

Length of both horns similar

Prehensile pointed lip

White rhinoceros

Larger and bigger, barrel-shaped body. Flat back, small hump.

The white rhino is a grazer. Mouth designed for gripping and tearing grass. Head mostly carried low to the ground.

Ears long and tubular

Front horn much longer

Broad, flat, wide lip

Some rare animal sightings

The African wild cat (left), the serval (middle) and the caracal (right) are all cats. They are nocturnal, solitary and secretive, and are therefore not often seen.

Cape fox are nocturnal and stay in dens during the day.

The ground pangolin is endangered, solitary and nocturnal.

The aardwolf is nocturnal and stays in dens during the day

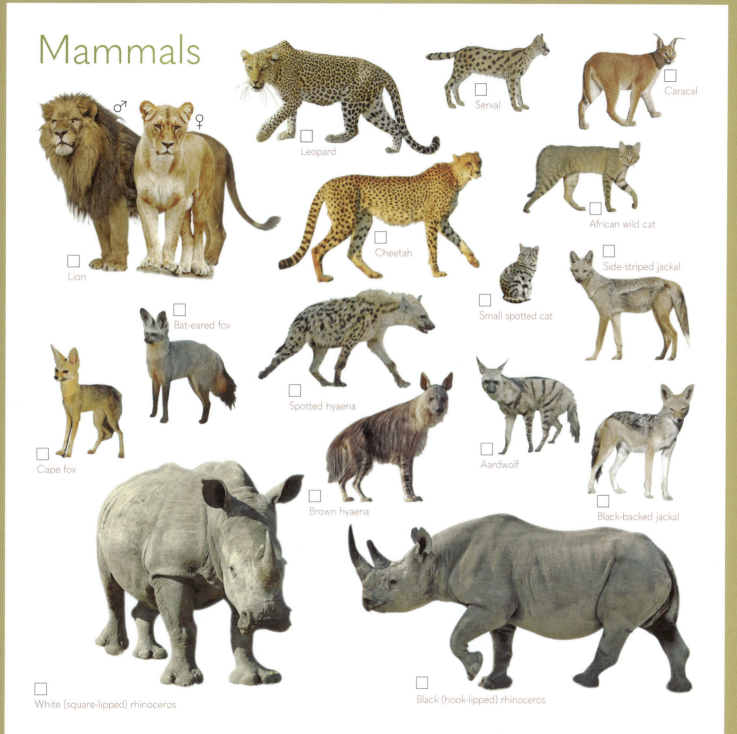

Birds

33

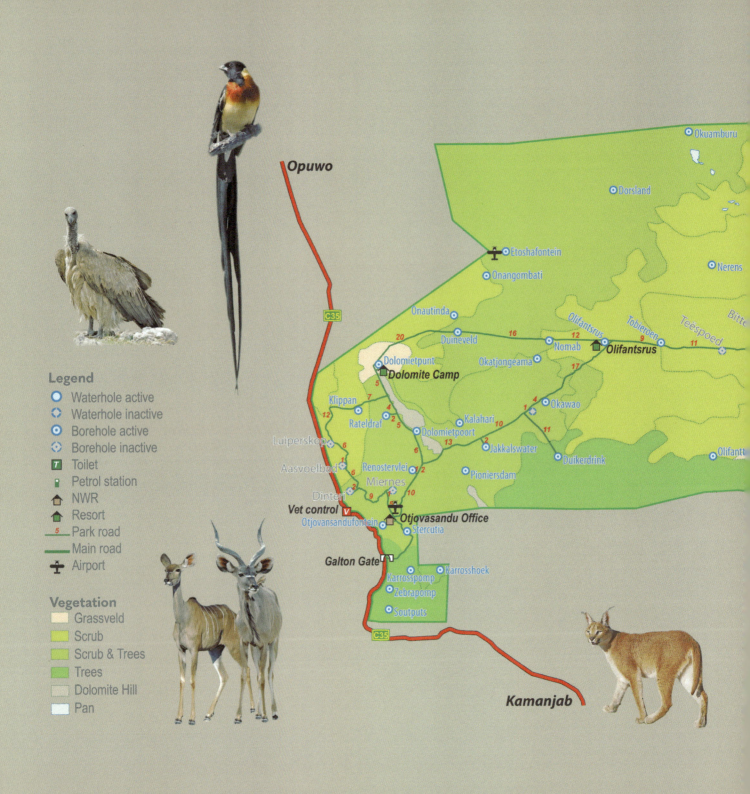

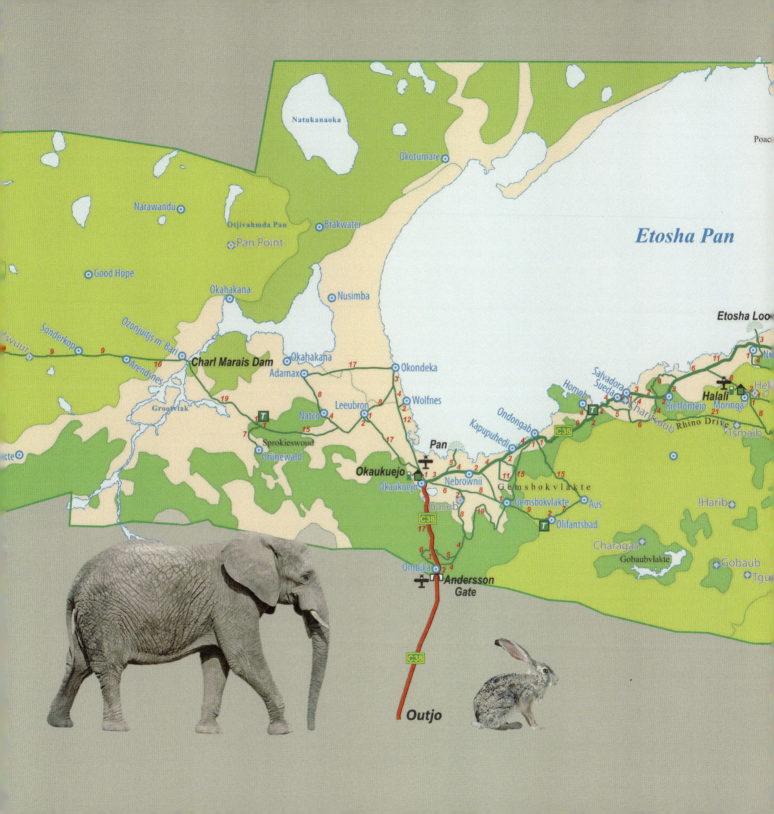

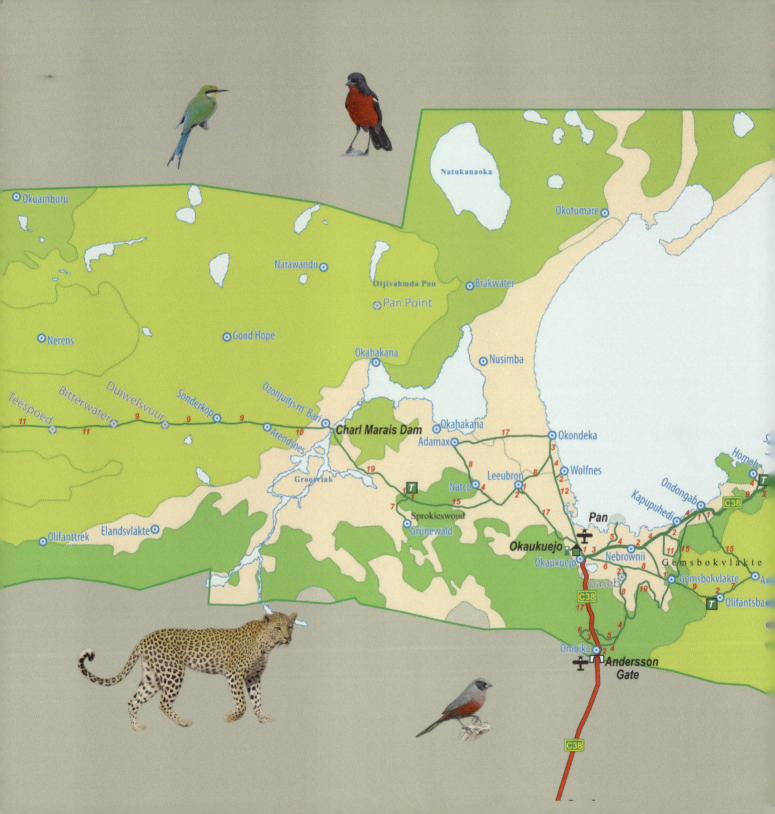

MAMMALS

Aardvark 34
Aardwolf 31
African civet 32
African elephant 32
African wild cat 31
Banded mongoose 34
Bat-eared fox 31
Black (hook-lipped)
    rhinoceros 31
Black-backed jackal 31
Black-faced impala 33
Blue wildebeest 33
Brown hyaena 31
Burchell's zebra 32
Cape fox 31
Cape hare 34
Cape porcupine 34
Caracal 31
Cheetah 31
Common duiker 33
Common eland 33
Common warthog 32
Damara dik-dik 33
Dwarf mongoose 34
Giraffe 32
Greater kudu 33
Ground pangolin 34
Hartmann's zebra 32
Honey badger 32
Klipspringer 33
Leopard 31
Lion 31
Red hartebeest 33
Rock dassie (Hyrax) 34
Scrub hare 34
Serval 31
Side-striped jackal 31
Slender mongoose 34
Small spotted cat 31
Small-spotted genet 34
South African ground
    squirrel 34
South African springhare 34
Southern African hedgehog 32
Southern lesser galago 32
Southern oryx 33
Spotted hyaena 31
Springbok 33
Steenbok 33
Suricate (Meerkat) 34
Tree squirrel 34
White (square-lipped)
    rhinoceros 31
Yellow mongoose 34

BIRDS

Abdim's stork 37
Acacia pied barbet 42
African darter 38
African golden oriole 41
African grey hornbill 37
African harrier-hawk 35
African hawk-eagle 35
African hoopoe 41
African jacana 38
African openbill 37
African paradise flycatcher .42
African pipit 39
African red-eyed bulbul 42
African sacred ibis 38
African scops owl 35
African spoonbill 38
African wattled lapwing 36
Ant-eating chat 42
Ashy tit 40
Bare-cheeked babbler 40
Barn swallow 42
Barred wren-warbler 39
Bateleur 35
Bearded woodpecker 41
Black crake 38
Black-backed puffback 40
Black-chested prinia 39
Black-chested snake eagle 35
Black-faced waxbill 39
Black-headed heron 38
Black-throated canary 39
Black-winged kite 35
Black-winged stilt 37
Blacksmith lapwing 36
Blue crane 38
Blue waxbill 39
Booted eagle 35
Bronze-winged courser 37
Brown-crowned tchagra 40
Brubru 40
Burchell's courser 37
Burchell's starling 41
Cape bunting 39
Cape crow 40
Cape penduline tit 40
Cape sparrow 39
Cape starling 41
Cape teal 38
Cape wagtail 39
Capped wheatear 42
Cardinal woodpecker 41
Caspian plover 37
Chat flycatcher 42
Chestnut weaver 40
Chestnut-banded plover 37
Chestnut-vented warbler ...39
Common buttonquail 36
Common buzzard 35
Common fiscal 41
Common greenshank 37
Common moorhen 38
Common ostrich 37
Common sandpiper 37
Common scimitarbill 41
Common waxbill 39
Crested francolin 36
Crimson-breasted shrike 40
Crowned lapwing 36
Damara red-billed hornbill .37
Desert cisticola 39
Diederik cuckoo 41
Double-banded courser 37
Double-banded sandgrouse 36
Dusky sunbird 42
Egyptian goose 38
European bee-eater 40
Familiar chat 42
Fawn-coloured lark 39
Fork-tailed drongo 41
Gabar goshawk 35
Glossy ibis 38
Golden-breasted bunting ...39
Golden-tailed woodpecker .41
Graukopfkasarka 38
Great egret 38
Great sparrow 39
Great spotted cuckoo ...41
Great white pelican 38
Greater flamingo 38
Greater kestrel 35
Greater painted-snipe 37
Greater striped swallow 42
Green wood hoopoe 41
Green-winged pytilia 40
Grey go-away-bird 41
Grey heron 38
Grey-backed camaroptera ..39
Grey-backed sparrow-lark ..39
Grey-headed kingfisher 42
Groundscraper thrush 42
Hamerkop 38
Hartlaub's spurfowl 36
Helmeted guineafowl 36
Jacobin cuckoo 41
Kalahari scrub robin 42
Kittlitz's plover 37
Knob-billed duck 38
Kori bustard 37
Lanner falcon 35
Lappet-faced vulture 36
Lark-like bunting 39
Laughing dove 41
Lesser flamingo 38
Lesser grey shrike 40
Lesser masked weaver 40
Lilac-breasted roller 41
Little egret 38
Little grebe 38
Little sparrowhawk 35
Long-tailed paradise
    whydah 39
Ludwig's bustard 36
Marabou stork 37
Marico flycatcher 42
Marico sunbird 42
Martial eagle 35
Meyer's parrot 41
Monteiro's hornbill 37
Namaqua dove 41
Namaqua sandgrouse 36
Northern black korhaan ...36
Orange river francolin 36
Pale-winged starling 41
Pearl-spotted owlet 35
Pied avocet 38
Pied crow 40
Pied kingfisher 42
Pin-tailed whydah 39
Pink-billed lark 39
Pririt batis 39
Purple heron 38
Purple roller 41
Pygmy falcon 35
Rattling cisticola 39
Red-backed shrike 40
Red-billed buffalo weaver 40
Red-billed quelea 40
Red-billed spurfowl 36
Red-billed teal 38
Red-capped lark 39
Red-crested korhaan 36
Red-faced mousebird 42
Red-headed finch 40
Red-knobbed coot 38
Red-necked falcon 35
Reed cormorant 38
Ring-necked dove 41
Rock kestrel 35
Rock martin 42
Rosy-faced lovebird 41
Ruff 37
Rufous-eared warbler 39
Rufous-naped lark 39
Rüppell's parrot 41
Sabota lark 39
Scaly-feathered weaver 40
Scarlet-chested sunbird 42
Secretarybird 36
Shaft-tailed whydah 39
Shikra 35
Short-toed rock-thrush 42
Sociable weaver 40
South African shelduck 38
Southern grey-headed
    sparrow 39
Southern masked weaver 40
Southern pale chanting
    goshawk 35
Southern pied babbler 40
Southern red-billed
    hornbill 37
Southern white-crowned
    shrike 40
Southern white-faced owl 35
Southern yellow-billed
    hornbill 37
Speckled pigeon 41
Spike-heeled lark 39
Spotted eagle owl 35
Spotted flycatcher 42
Spotted thick-knee 36
Squacco heron 38
Steppe eagle 35
Striped kingfisher 42
Swainson's spurfowl 36
Swallow-tailed bee-eater 40
Tawny eagle 35
Temminck's courser 37
Three-banded plover 37
Verreaux's eagle 35
Violet wood hoopoe 41
Violet-backed starling 41
Violet-eared waxbill 39
Wahlberg's eagle 35
Water thick-knee 36
Wattled starling 41
Western barn owl 35
Western cattle egret 38
Whiskered tern 38
White stork 37
White-backed mousebird 42
White-backed vulture 36
White-bellied sunbird 42
White-breasted cormorant ..38
White-browed scrub robin ..42
White-browed
    sparrow-weaver 40
White-crested
    helmetshrike 40
White-fronted plover .....
White-headed vulture 36
White-throated canary 39
White-winged tern 38
Willow warbler 39
Wood sandpiper 37
Yellow canary 39
Yellow-bellied eremomela ..39
Yellow-billed kite 35
Yellow-billed stork 37

REPTILES

Bicoloured quill-snouted
    snake 43
Black mamba 43
Boomslang 43
Brown house snake 43
Cape cobra 43
Common marsh terrapin 43
Dwarf beaked snake 43
Eastern tiger snake 43
Horned adder 43
Kalahari tent tortoise 43
Leopard tortoise 43
Mole snake 43
Olive grass snake 43
Puff adder 43
Rock monitor 43
Shield cobra 43
Southern African python 43
Southern/bibron's
    burrowing asp 43
Spotted bush snake 43
Striped skaapsteker 43
Western barred
    spitting cobra 43
Western stripe-bellied sand
    snake 43
Zebra cobra 43

46

Printed in Great Britain
by Amazon